Both Sides of the Plate

Insider Secrets for Navigating the College Baseball Recruiting Process

Rick Allen, Founder

edited by
Julie Allen, Co-Founder

www.InformedAthlete.com

The Allen Group, Inc.
PO Box 52125
Tulsa, OK 74152

Phone: 918-994-7272
Email: rick@informedathlete.com
Website: www.informedathlete.com

Limits of Liability and Disclaimer of Warranty
The author and publisher shall not be liable for your misuse of this material. This book is strictly for informational and educational purposes.

Warning – Disclaimer
The purpose of this book is to educate and entertain. The author and/or publisher do not guarantee that anyone following these techniques, suggestions, tips, ideas, or strategies will become successful. The author and/or publisher shall have neither liability nor responsibility to anyone with respect to any loss or damage caused, or alleged to be caused, directly or indirectly by the information contained in this book.

ISBN: 978-0-615-35853-6

Testimonials

"Rick Allen has been a wonderful resource for our family to help us understand what our son must do to ensure compliance with the numerous academic and athletic rules that apply to him as a collegiate athlete.

Because of Rick's background as a compliance officer with a major university, he was able to help guide us through the issues involved of moving from a D1 to a Junior College and back to a D1 university to ensure NCAA rules were not violated and to give us good information on the various options available to our son.

Through our experiences, we have come to learn to value Rick's opinion and have realized that it is difficult, if not impossible, to try and interpret the many rules and regulations that govern NCAA athletes unless you have a helping hand."

- Parent of a Big 12 baseball player

My wife and I are certain that without your guidance in explaining the NCAA rules and the steps involved in requesting a release, our son's meeting with the coach would not have resulted in the desired outcome. Many current and former student athletes have since contacted us and expressed their amazement that our son's request was granted because when they asked for a release, they were simply told "No."

- Parents of a Division I football player

"Our daughter is on a full athletic scholarship. We were told that her fifth year would be paid for. However, this year she took a medical redshirt because of a shoulder injury. She would still have two years of eligibility. The question arose would the fifth year still be paid in full as the previous year because she plans to play that final year?

We contacted Rick Allen for advice & he responded to our query very quickly and professionally. He noted that she should receive the same full ride as the year before. If there was a problem and we were notified that the amount would be anything less, Mr. Allen advised that we should petition the review board for the full amount. This was a relief because at least we knew that we had an option for action on our part, if needed."

- Parent of an ACC softball player

"Over the years that I have known Rick, he has provided us assistance working through recruitment issues, providing questions to present to coaches, etc. We never needed his direction more than the Fall of 2008. Our son was attending an NAIA institution on scholarship, and informed us that he was unhappy with the program and wanted to seek other opportunities.

Rick provided us the guidance to allow our son to obtain the release from the NAIA school and open discussions with an NCAA Division II school. Our son is now attending and playing for the NCAA Division II, with a better scholarship and better attitude. We couldn't be happier or more appreciative of Rick's assistance."

-Parents of a Division II Baseball Player

"**Informed Athlete** provides accurate, reliable information to coaches, student-athletes and their families and is the only resource of its kind to my knowledge. I have known Rick Allen for years and still to this day contact him when I have questions regarding specific situations and details."

Josh Holliday
Assistant Baseball Coach
Vanderbilt University

"I think it's a much needed service. I see many kids make bad decisions based on a lack of information and education."

Billy Gasparino
National Cross Checker – Toronto Blue Jays

"Rick Allen was solely responsible for my quickened transition to OSU in 1999. I attribute that assistance to his extended knowledge of NCAA policy and academics. With www.informedathlete.com that knowledge is passed on directly to the student-athlete and the parents."

Neb Brown
Former Oklahoma State University baseball player
Arizona Diamondbacks 2002 11th round draft choice

"Rick Allen is an absolute expert in his field. When it comes to NCAA rules and regulations, he's as good as it gets."

Jerry Ford
Founder & President
Perfect Game USA

Dedication

To my wife, Julie, who has provided the editing for this book, I would not have been able to complete this without your assistance and contributions. Thank you so much for your years of love and support. With the personal experiences that we can share through Informed Athlete and with your marketing expertise, the journey with this new venture will be very exciting.

To our son, Ryan, we are so impressed with the maturity you have shown through some trying times and how you have grown into such a great young man. Pursue your dreams with passion, and be sure to remember those friends and mentors who believe in you.

To all of the parents who we have talked to over the years, and who we will be talking to in the future, we have felt your excitement and we have felt your heartache. We know that "it's just a game" but when it's your son or daughter that is involved, it's much more than that.

A Note from the Author

Each year, millions of kids compete in some form of competitive athletics with the goal of earning a college athletic scholarship. Parents spend thousands of dollars on lessons, equipment, competitive sports teams, and travel in the hopes that their child will be noticed by college recruiters and offered an athletic scholarship to play their chosen sport.

However, an athletic skill is just one side of the equation to earning a college athletic scholarship. Understanding and navigating efficiently through the rules of the athletic recruiting process is a complex task and often results in unrealistic expectations with disappointing results.

What we do is educate, advise and assist families of high school and college student-athletes on issues related to athletic recruiting, academic eligibility, transfer issues and financial aid rules so that they are able to make informed decisions that are in their best interest.

For over 25 years, I worked on two major college campuses specializing in NCAA compliance: the University of Illinois from 1981-1997 and at Oklahoma State University from 1997 to 2006.

As Vice-President of Compliance for JumpForward (a company developing technology for college and university athletic departments) and previously as a consultant with The Compliance Group, I continue to maintain close contact with athletic departments throughout the United States.

In addition to my professional experience, **I have walked in your shoes** and gained first-hand understanding from a parent's perspective when our son was recruited to a Big 12 institution and received an athletic scholarship.

Through all my years sitting in bleachers and traveling to watch our own son, parents frequently asked me questions related to their sons or daughters.

My wife and I started **Informed Athlete** in 2008 as a way to educate and advise families and student-athletes through what can be very complicated, confusing, and often-times overwhelming situations.

If you have a story that you are willing to share that may help other families in the future (we will be sure to keep you anonymous if you prefer), send it along and we can include it on our website, in a webcast, or perhaps in our next book!

Rick Allen, Founder
www.InformedAthlete.com

Table of contents

Introduction

There are hundreds of books, videos, camps, and coaches to help your child develop the athletic skills that will help them excel in their chosen sport. There are also a number of books talking about what you need to do to be recruited and how to be seen.

This book is different. This book provides real-life advice and experiences that share some of the many situations you will encounter if you are actively pursuing an athletic scholarship.

My personal experience as the parent of a student-athlete who was recruited to a Big 12 school on an athletic scholarship, as well as my professional experience with over 20 years of responsibility for NCAA rules at two major universities – Oklahoma State University and the University of Illinois – make me uniquely qualified to advise parents, athletes and coaches on issues involving recruiting, eligibility, financial aid, and transfer issues.

In this book, I give real-life examples of how important it is to be an **Informed Athlete** starting with the recruiting process and moving through the college experience.

Decisions made during the recruiting process can have HUGE and lasting impact both emotionally and financially later on.

Some of the stories I share are based on situations I've encountered throughout my years on campus.

Some of these stories include mistakes that were made in our own son's recruitment process despite my years of NCAA experience and expertise.

It's our hope that sharing some of them with you will hopefully make a difference for your son or daughter.

Chapter 1 - Getting an Early Start in the Recruiting Process

"You've got to be very careful if you don't know where you are going because you might not get there." Yogi Berra

One of the most frequent questions that parents ask me is how early their son or daughter should start attending recruiting or "showcase" events. Or, "What types of events should I be taking them to?" There are probably many different opinions depending upon who you talk to, but here are my thoughts.

Athletes should start getting out to recruiting or "showcase" events no later than their sophomore year, and perhaps even their freshman year. Some of this depends upon how physically mature they are, and how their skill level compares to others their age, or in the grade above them.

As I travel to college campuses to consult with college athletic departments regarding their NCAA rules compliance programs, I have the opportunity to speak to coaches of various sports at the NCAA Division I and II level, as well as colleges who have been in the NAIA, and are transitioning to join the NCAA.

Coaches are telling me that they are completing their recruiting earlier than in years past. The trend appears to be growing as the comments are consistent from coaches at colleges from the east coast, down to Texas, and out to the west coast.

When I conduct compliance reviews for college athletic departments, one of the questions that I always ask them is how they monitor their recruiting phone calls to ensure that they don't violate NCAA rules.

Division I coaches in most sports are not allowed to place recruiting phone calls until the July 1 following a prospect's junior year of high school (June 15 for Division II coaches).

A number of coaches have said that by the time they reach July 1st following the junior year of that particular recruiting class, their recruiting for that class is almost finished, and they already have their commitments. They state that "the phone calls we make are just to maintain the relationship that we already have through e-mail (which can start during the junior year of high school) or through discussions during their visits to our campus."

Our son played high school baseball with a talented player who was highly regarded in the state at his position. Yet, he was not highly recruited. Part of the reason is because he was from a college town, and there was a perception that was difficult to overcome. The perception was held by coaches of other college baseball teams that the player would probably just end up attending the local college and playing for them.

However, another reason that this player was not highly recruited is because he didn't attend many recruiting showcase events. He played a lot of traveling youth baseball as he was growing up, but once in high school, he mainly played high school ball, and American Legion baseball.

While American Legion baseball is certainly a good organization and has a long and rich tradition, in many parts of the country it is not the place to "be seen" for young baseball players looking to be recruited.

Baseball players need to be participating in recruiting showcase events, or playing on quality summer teams which travel across a region of the country (if not further) to participate in tournaments with and against other quality players.

The end result for the young man mentioned above is that he did not gain a large amount of recruiting interest, ended up playing for the local college team, did not get a lot of playing time, and walked away from college baseball while he still had eligibility remaining.

In cases where this happens, I admire players for admitting that they don't have the passion or desire to play college ball anymore and that they are ready to move on to the next phase in their life.

But, at the same time, in cases like this one, I always wonder how things might have turned out if the young man had gotten an opportunity at another college through increased recruiting opportunities, or had been willing to go to a two-year college first to get more exposure to four-year colleges.

Getting started early will put your son or daughter "on the radar" of college coaches so that there is name recognition or name awareness when they are observed at other events as they get older.

* Keep in mind that coaches share a lot of information with other coaches, and in the sport of baseball, also share a lot of information with pro scouts.

* Getting started early will aid with the name recognition and also open up other opportunities, such as invitations to try out for premier traveling baseball teams or to participate in events such as local or regional tryouts for the Area Code Games.

What about baseball camps held by colleges and universities on their campuses? Should you spend your money to go to those types of events? I believe this depends upon a couple of factors.

One is whether this is a school that you would seriously consider attending, and would it be a good fit for you academically and athletically?

For example, if you are an athlete who is a good, but not a great student academically, consider whether Duke or Stanford would be a good fit for you, even if you perform well at their baseball camp and the coaches are seriously interested in you as a baseball player.

The other factor I believe you should consider is whether there will be coaches from other schools there to help out at the camp, and if so, how many?

* Coaches often employ coaches from other colleges to work their camps. For example, they might employ a few coaches from two-year colleges that they normally recruit from, as a means of repaying a favor to the coach.

Or they may employ coaches who are currently at other schools, but are former players or assistant coaches at their college or university.

If you are considering attending a camp on a college campus, you may want to ask if other coaches will be working the camp, how many, and what schools they are from, or what schools have been represented in past camp sessions.

Chapter 2 - What if I didn't get an early start, and I'm still receiving little or no recruiting interest?

"The game isn't over until it's over." Yogi Berra

Parents, as well as their athletes, often express frustration that they are not getting much, if any, recruiting interest, while other athletes that they have competed with and against are receiving lots of recruiting interest.

This happened with our own son and so I have experienced this first hand.

In the summer after his junior year, our son played on a traveling summer team that competed in the Oklahoma-Kansas region, and he also attended a couple of baseball camps on college campuses.

He had performed well in front of college coaches on at least five different college campuses, hitting well at some venues and throwing a complete game in July heat at another.

⊁Yet, when the July 1st date for colleges to start making recruiting phone calls to upcoming seniors rolled around, he didn't receive any recruiting calls. And this continued through the early fall.

He did receive some phone calls from two–year colleges who were inviting him to visit campus, but no calls from four-year schools.

Two events during the fall of his senior year, as well as help from the coaches of his fall team were instrumental, and both of the events happened to be *Perfect Game* events.

The Midwest Top Prospect Showcase in Iowa, although one of the smaller *Perfect Game* events, exposed him to coaches in the upper Midwest that he had not had exposure to previously.

And the Fall team that he played on participated in the World Wood Bat Championship in Jupiter, Florida. Through the additional exposure at *Perfect Game* events, he did begin to receive recruiting interest midway through his senior year.

So, what things should an athlete do if they are in the midst of their senior year and have not yet received a lot of recruiting interest? Here are a few:

1. **Determine who your best advocate is**. Find someone who believes in you and will promote you to college coaches. (In the case of our son, while the high school coach was helpful, it was "cold calls" to college coaches by the coaches of his Fall team that got results.)

2. **Draft a letter or e-mail to send to college coaches** telling them how you can make their team better. This is often more effective than a resume sent to coaches by a recruiting service. I know this because I saw what happened to those resumes when I worked in a college athletic department. Many of them went directly in the trash can with no coach reading them.

3. **Make a video to send to college coaches** as an e-mail attachment, on a DVD, or as a YouTube video. (For our son, we used the services of Skillshow which was available at the site of the *Perfect Game* event that he attended.) The video may tweak their interest to contact you or your coaches to request more information, or, in some cases, they may pass along your name to a friend at another school, perhaps an area two-year college, or a college where one of their former assistant coaches just became the head coach.

One of the things to keep in mind if you are in this situation and it is the middle of your senior year, and you have not yet gotten a lot of recruiting interest, is to discern who is really interested and to what level they are interested.

I can illustrate this point through the following story which was recently shared with me.

I'll call this player "David" to protect his real identity. David received all-state recognition as an outfielder for his high school baseball team. He was also a pitcher, but his best talent was as a hitter and outfielder.

David was recruited late to the college that signed him. In one of the games that the college team saw him play following his junior year of high school, David hit two home runs. He did not pitch in any of the games that his future college team observed.

However, when he arrived on campus for his freshman year, David was not even issued a bat, and was told that "you are a pitcher from this point on."

He transferred to another school after his freshman year for a number of reasons, but obviously having the bat taken out of his hands was one of the major reasons.

So, while David was excited to be recruited and offered a scholarship to this school, in hindsight, I'm sure that he would tell you that he should have asked the following questions:

1. What position did you recruit me for? What role do you see for me?
2. Who on your staff has seen me play, and which of my games did you observe?
3. Who else provided information about me, was it my high school coach, a summer team coach, or an area scout?

If you really want to play at the college level and you have not received much recruiting interest, don't give up hope, and keep an open mind about opportunities that may exist.

Two situations that occurred at our son's high school illustrate these possibilities.

One of our son's high school teammates had attended a few recruiting events during the summer prior to his senior year, and during the fall of senior year, but had received little recruiting interest even as late as the end of his senior baseball season and approaching high school graduation. He was a very good hitter, but there were questions about what position he would play at the college level.

Surprisingly, late in his senior year, the high school coach received a phone call from a coach who had just been hired at a small college in the state, and was trying to find some players to fill his roster.

The college coach told the high school coach: *"I was just hired last week and I don't know how many players are returning from last year, so I'm holding an open tryout next week. Do you have anybody you can send to the tryout?"*

This player attended the open tryout, and was offered a substantial scholarship, even though he had received little recruiting interest from any colleges up to that point.

More recently, one of our newsletter subscribers shared the following story about her son who was getting ready to head off to college:

"Greg (not his real name) sat the bench the majority of the year. He only pitched more than one inning in two games all season. At those two crucial games, however, scouts were sitting in the stands. These scouts told their college coach friends about Greg's size, ability, and potential. At the end of the season, he was invited for several campus visits/tryouts, and he was offered scholarships at all but one. He accepted baseball/academic scholarships at an NAIA school."

While these stories are certainly not the norm in recruiting, they do illustrate that opportunities can appear unexpectedly at any time.

Chapter Three – Visiting Campus

"You can observe a lot just by watching." Yogi Berra

One of the best ways to learn about the schools and athletic programs that you are interested in is to visit campus.

From the standpoint of NCAA rules, there are **"official visits"** and **"unofficial visits"** which will be briefly explained a bit later, but for now it seems more important to focus on what to ask and what to look for when visiting campus.

But, before we get to that point, however, there are some things that you can look for by viewing the athletic website and looking up information regarding the baseball program. The information may be easily found on the website under current information, as well as the "Archives" section, or you may desire to download or view a PDF of the team's official media guide.

Here are a few of the things that you can look for on the website:

1. What is the ratio of incoming freshman each year compared to transfer athletes? Does it appear that the coaches build their program by relying mostly on high-school talent, or do they pursue "quick fixes" by bringing in a lot of transfers from other college programs?

    Neither is necessarily a bad approach. However, you may want to consider whether you hope to be recruited with other freshman that you can build a lifelong friendship with over three or four years of being teammates, or whether you are ok with going to a program that recruits transfers who may only be in the program for one year before they move on to professional baseball?

2. What is the history of playing time for freshmen? How many at-bats or innings do they get in their first year?

3. How has the program developed players at your position during their time at the school? Is there a general progression of increasing at-bats and innings as players' experience increases?

In the case of our son and his baseball recruitment, we did most of these things before visiting campus. We knew that the program did not normally recruit many transfers unless they had specific holes to fill in a particular year. In most cases, they relied on recruiting high school players and developing them over three or four years.

But what is more important is asking lots of questions when on campus for a visit. This is where some of our biggest mistakes were made.

I can tell you that even after over 25 years of experience in college athletic departments, and working closely with NCAA rules for 20 of those years, there are a number of things that I regret about our experience in the recruiting process, and the questions that we should have asked on some of our visits are some of the biggest.

Without going into great detail, here are a few of the questions that we should have asked, or things that we should have done differently, and that you need to do correctly to avoid our mistakes:

※ 1. Be sure to make a good connection with the head coach. It may be that you are being recruited by the top recruiting assistant on the staff, but keep in mind that it is ultimately the head coach who decides who is in the lineup each day and how many opportunities each player is going to get.

2. Ask players (not just the one that may have been hand-picked to host you, but players who will soon be leaving the program and may feel a bit more free to comment) whether they would choose to attend the school if they had to do it over again. Why or why not?

3. What is the relationship of coaches (head and assistant) with players away from the playing field? Does the coaching staff care about the players as individuals away from the field? Can players freely sit down with the coaches in their offices to shoot the breeze or to watch an inning of a game on the office TV?

NCAA Official and Unofficial Visits

The NCAA rules define "official visits" and "unofficial visits." Let's review unofficial visits first, as they are simpler to explain.

Any time an athlete visits campus with friends, or with parents or other family members, at their own expense, this is an *"unofficial"* **visit**.

✱ During an **unofficial visit**, the college or university can provide up to three complimentary admissions to attend a campus sporting event so that the athlete can take in a bit of the campus atmosphere when an event is held on campus.

The college cannot provide any other expenses, such as a meal, overnight lodging or a reimbursement of travel expenses. (NCAA Division II institutions are permitted to provide a recruit, and the recruits relatives or legal guardians, with one meal during an unofficial visit.)

An athlete can make an unofficial visit to campus as early as their freshman or sophomore year of high school if they choose to do so. Some families visit a campus during the summer as part of a summer vacation or weekend trip, and try to get a feel for the campus when nobody knows they are coming and they are not being given a "sales pitch."

Official **visits**, on the other hand, are:

1. Highly regulated by NCAA rules,

2. Cannot occur earlier than the first day of classes for an athletes' senior year of high school, and

3. The athlete must be registered with the NCAA Eligibility Center and must submit a high school transcript and ACT or SAT test scores before they will be allowed to make an official visit to a campus.

During an official visit to an NCAA institution, it is permissible for the institution to provide a prospect with transportation to visit the campus, and with meals and lodging during a visit to campus that cannot exceed 48 hours from the time that the prospect (and parents or legal guardians, if they accompany the prospect) arrives on campus.

Large universities with ample recruiting budgets will often provide all of the permissible expenses that they are permitted by rule to provide.

However, some institutions, especially smaller colleges or universities with limited recruiting budgets, may only provide meals while on campus, or meals and lodging for just one night instead of two.

If you are invited to make an official visit to campus, I strongly urge you to take advantage of that offer. This is another mistake that we made in the baseball recruitment of our son.

We turned down the opportunity to make an official visit to a campus that was very interested in our son because he had already made up his mind that his first choice was the choice for him (for a variety of reasons that we agreed with at the time).

He felt it was not fair to accept an expense-paid official visit from the second school, when he had made up his mind that he wasn't going to go there, because he would not be seriously considering them.

At the time, I was very impressed with his ethics and his moral compass and thought that was a sensible decision. However, in looking back on that decision now, it was not a good decision from a business standpoint.

Had we gone on the official visit to the second institution, we would have been able to fairly compare facilities, atmosphere, personality of coaches, and other factors.

We also would have had a competing scholarship offer that we could have used for negotiating purposes in trying to obtain a better scholarship offer from his first institution of choice.

We would have also been able to more accurately determine the level of interest that each institution had in our son, rather than getting caught up in other factors such as the conference of each institution and the competitive level of play in the conference, the distance from home, and how often we would be able to see him play.

Chapter 4 - Eligibility

"Number one rule, attend to business" Lefty Grove

One of the main reasons that we started **Informed Athlete** is to educate and advise high school athletes and parents on the NCAA recruiting and eligibility rules.

In this chapter, I will provide not just information about NCAA eligibility rules, but will also include "real-life" stories that may be of interest.

And, while I'm sure the stories are more interesting than the rules, the rules can be confusing, so it may be best to start off by explaining some of the eligibility rules, and then follow up with the stories later.

Eligibility as an athlete upon initial enrollment at their college or university

Here is some information about the NCAA academic eligibility requirements that athletes must satisfy in high school to be immediately eligible for practice, competition, and athletic scholarships as a freshman. Athletes who achieve these standards to be immediately eligible as freshmen are considered "qualifiers."

NCAA Division I

1. Must complete 16 "core courses" which are broadly defined as college prep courses such as English, math, natural sciences, social sciences, etc. Two semesters of a course such as Biology constitute one "core course."

2. Must satisfy all high school graduation requirements for your respective school and state, and must graduate from the high school.

3. Must achieve a high school GPA that corresponds with a matching ACT sum score (the sum of scores on the four subparts of the ACT test) or SAT score on the critical reading and math portions of the SAT test (NCAA does not consider scores on the writing portion of the SAT test). This is a "sliding scale" which allows a student to offset a lower GPA with a higher ACT or SAT test score, or conversely, to offset a lower test score with a higher GPA. Here are a couple of examples: An athlete with a core course GPA of 2.500 requires an SAT score of 820 or a sum ACT score of 68, while an athlete with a core course GPA of 3.000 requires an SAT score of 620 or a sum ACT score of 52.

4. Official ACT and/or SAT test scores must be submitted to the NCAA Eligibility Center for determination of eligibility as a freshman, as well as an official high school transcript from each high school that the prospect has attended.

NCAA Division II

1. Must complete 14 "core courses" which are broadly defined as college prep courses such as English, math, natural sciences, social sciences, etc. Two semesters of a course such as Biology constitute one "core course." Athletes who enter college as freshmen in Fall 2013 will be required to take 16 "core courses."

2. Must achieve a minimum cumulative GPA of 2.000 in at least 14 core courses.

3. Need minimum SAT score of 820 or a sum ACT score of 68.

4. Must satisfy all high school graduation requirements for your respective school and state, and must graduate from the high school.

5. Official ACT and/or SAT test scores must be submitted to the NCAA Eligibility Center for determination of eligibility as a freshman, as well as an official high school transcript from each high school that the prospect has attended.

The rules cited above are the academic eligibility requirements for incoming freshmen in order to be immediately eligible to practice, compete, and receive an athletic scholarship at any NCAA Division I or II college or university respectively.

In addition, each freshman must have their amateur status certified by the Eligibility Center as well.

The following story may appear confusing because it regards the transfer situation of a baseball player from a two-year college to an NCAA Division I university, rather than an athlete who is going directly from high school to an NCAA Division I or II college.

The points that I am trying to illustrate with the following story are:

1. Athletes who are informed and achieve the NCAA academic requirements for freshman eligibility are "qualifiers." They have the opportunity to be immediately eligible to practice, compete and receive an athletic scholarship as a freshman if they choose to enroll at an NCAA Division I or II college or university as a freshman.

2. Even if these athletes choose to begin their college career at a two-year college and then transfer to an NCAA Division I or II college or university, the transfer can be easier when it comes time to transfer from the two-year college if they are a qualifier. This is because a qualifier does not have to satisfy as many requirements to be immediately eligible as a transfer student from a two-year college to NCAA Division I or II.

Now for the story:

In the Fall of 1999, Neb Brown and his father, Jim, came to see me when I was on the staff of the Oklahoma State University athletic department.

Neb had played his high school baseball at Chaparral High School in Scottsdale, Arizona. He then attended a two-year college in Arizona, and was now planning to transfer to OSU.

After reviewing his transcript to see if he would be eligible under the NCAA transfer rules, I determined that he would have to obtain a large number of additional hours in one semester at a two-year college before being able to transfer and be immediately eligible at Oklahoma State for the 2000 season, unless a waiver of the transfer rules was approved by the NCAA.

The tricky part about the situation is that he would not be able to practice with or play in any fall baseball games at the two-year college in order to preserve his opportunity to play immediately at OSU, due to season-of-competition rules.

If Neb had received proper guidance about NCAA eligibility requirements from somebody at his high school, or at the two-year college, his transfer situation could have been much smoother and he would have been able to transfer directly to Oklahoma State University without the need to "detour" to a second two-year college to gain additional hours for immediate eligibility.

Neb did successfully transfer to OSU, played two years, was drafted by the Arizona Diamondbacks, and ultimately reached the AAA level within their organization.

I also encountered similar transfer situations with many athletes who had attended a two-year college for one or two years and then hoped to transfer to Oklahoma State University and try out for the OSU football team as a "walk-on."

In many cases I had to inform them that they could not even try out because they did not have the proper academic credentials to satisfy the NCAA transfer rules.

The point that I want to stress in this section is that all high school athletes should try to achieve the NCAA Division I academic requirements noted earlier, because they then have the widest range of college choices available to them after they complete high school.

Many athletes who were not good academic students in high school still do go on and achieve many, if not all, of their academic and athletic goals.

However, their road to those goals will quite often be easier if they can satisfy the Division I initial eligibility requirements. This is because they will not be as restricted in their transfer requirements as they will be if they are considered an NCAA "non-qualifier."

NCAA Division III

Division III colleges and universities do not have required national standards that must be met by high school prospective student-athletes in order to be immediately eligible for NCAA practice and competition.

Eligibility for athletic scholarships is not an issue at Division III because they are not permitted, although academic scholarships are quite common at Division III and can be quite substantial.

The only requirement for NCAA Division III initial eligibility is that the prospective student-athlete be admitted to the institution in the same manner as the general student population.

NAIA Academic Requirements

Here is information about NAIA immediate eligibility requirements for incoming freshmen:

1. An entering freshman student must be a graduate of an accredited high school or be accepted as a regular student in good standing as defined by the enrolling institution.

2. An entering freshman student must meet two of three entry-level requirements:
    a. A minimum composite score of 18 on the ACT or an 860 on the Critical Reading and Math sections of the SAT.
    b. An overall high school GPA of 2.000 or higher on a 4.000 scale.
    c. Graduate in the upper half of the student's high school graduating class.

Note about NAIA freshman eligibility – the NAIA will be establishing an NAIA Eligibility Center to review and determine initial eligibility for all athletes that wish to be certified eligible for athletic participation at NAIA institutions for competition beginning in the 2011-12 academic year.

NJCAA Academic Requirements

Here is information about Junior College eligibility requirements for incoming freshmen:

1. An entering freshman student must be a graduate of a high school with an academic diploma or a General Education diploma.

2. Non-high school graduates can establish eligibility for athletic participation by completing one term of college study passing 12 credits with a 1.75 grade point average or higher.

Note: Two-year colleges in California are not governed by the NJCAA, but by the California Community College Athletic Association. The CCCAA academic requirements are similar.

Playing eligibility once enrolled at an NCAA Division I or II institution

So far in this chapter, we have discussed the eligibility requirements for immediate eligibility for prospective student-athletes first arriving at their college or university, and have briefly talked about how those eligibility requirements affect transfer athletes.

I would like to briefly note NCAA rules for playing eligibility and what constitutes the use of a season of eligibility at the NCAA Division I and II level, as I believe this is important information for both freshman and transfer student-athletes.

Basically, the rule is quite simple. **Student-athletes are allowed four seasons of competition.** Any amount of participation in actual game competition will constitute the use of a season of eligibility.

At NCAA Division I, the four seasons of competition must be used within what is commonly referred to as the "five-year clock." Student-athletes have five years from the date of their first full-time enrollment at any college-level institution to utilize their four seasons of competition.

The rule for NCAA Division II is a bit different. Division II utilizes the "10-semester" rule. The four seasons of eligibility for Division II must be used within the first 10 full-time semesters of the student-athletes' collegiate enrollment.

So, the key difference is that if an athlete chooses not to attend college for a semester for whatever reason - perhaps there is an illness in the family, or perhaps they are working to earn additional money to pay for college – that semester will not count against them at the Division II level, but it will keep counting toward the "five-year clock" under Division I rules.

The other important point to remember is that any amount of participation in actual competition will constitute the use of a season of eligibility.

This is especially important for athletes to understand if they are considering utilizing a "redshirt" season to gain size and strength in the weight room, or to improve their skill level.

nletes considering the use of a redshirt season should have a thoughtful discussion with the coach to try to determine how the coach intends to use them in the upcoming season.

For example, if a baseball player comes off the bench to pinch hit or pinch run one time, or if a relief pitcher comes in and throws one pitch to get the game-ending double play, that player has used a full season of eligibility, even if that is their only participation for the whole season.

An upset parent recently related such a story to me. An athlete had one at bat, yet he did not have any injury, serious illness, or any other unusual circumstance that would warrant a waiver of NCAA rules, so he used a season of eligibility despite getting to the plate only one time.

Perhaps a discussion with the head coach about his expectations for the season would have caused the athlete to request redshirting for the season, or might have given him the option to consider a 4-2-4 transfer (which will be discussed in Chapter 6).

Chapter Five – Athletic Scholarships

"A nickel ain't worth a dime anymore."
Yogi Berra

"Our ____ (fill in the blank with son, daughter, neighbor, cousin, etc.) just received a full ride!!"

How many times have you heard a comment like that, or seen one on an internet message board, or in a newspaper article to describe an athlete who has been offered an athletic scholarship?

It is very exciting to be offered an athletic scholarship, but the majority of the time, the scholarship is not a "full ride." And, it is not guaranteed for four years, as some people would have you believe!

First of all, let me explain that in NCAA-speak, all sports are separated into one of two categories when it comes to athletic scholarships: sports are classified as either *"head-count"* sports, or *"equivalency"* sports.

Each athlete who is receiving an athletic scholarship in any amount is considered a "counter." In a head-count sport, each counter is assumed to be receiving a full athletic scholarship.

The following NCAA Division I sports are head-count sports: men's and women's basketball, football, women's gymnastics, women's tennis, and women's volleyball.

All other NCAA Division I sports, as well as all Division II sports and NAIA sports, are considered "equivalency" sports. This is because coaches in those sports can divide the scholarships among multiple team members, as long as they don't exceed their team "equivalency" when the total scholarships for all team members are added together.

For example, Division I baseball is permitted to provide no more than 11.7 total scholarships, but they can divide those among their team members, so that one athlete may be receiving a 60% scholarship while another is receiving a 25% scholarship.

Note: At the end of this chapter, I will include a listing of some of the more popular NCAA sports and the maximum scholarships they are permitted to provide.

The NCAA defines a "full grant-in-aid" as the value of tuition and course-related fees, room and board, and the value of books, as determined by the financial aid office on each campus.

Not all fees and expenses are included, so that even an athlete on a "full ride" will still have out-of-pocket expenses for things like a parking permit or supplies for class.

The other key point that athletes and parents should keep in mind is that athletic scholarships can only be awarded for one year at a time. There is no such thing as a "multi-year" athletic scholarship.

Coaches may say that they guarantee a scholarship for four or five years, and their history may show that most of their athletes have received their athletic scholarships for all or five years of their eligibility.

However, the NCAA only permits schools to award scholarships for one year at a time. Each athlete must be notified by July 1 each year whether their athletic scholarship will be renewed for the following year.

And, the difficult part for many athletes and parents to understand is that coaches can choose to reduce or cancel the scholarship for the upcoming year for almost any reason they choose.

The NCAA requires member institutions to make a hearing opportunity available to any athlete whose athletic scholarship has been reduced or cancelled, and the information about the hearing opportunity must be included in the written notice that informs the athlete of the reduction or cancellation.

In most cases, the athlete chooses not to appeal the decision because they plan to transfer and move on to another school.

However, in those cases in which the athlete does appeal the reduction or cancellation, their appeal is often denied as the appeal committee will uphold the decision of the coach and athletic department.

This happens to many athletes, despite the promise when they are being recruited that their scholarship will never go down or be taken away as long as they conduct themselves in the proper manner on and off the field.

I used to work for an athletic director who believed that if coaches made a mistake in recruiting and awarding athletic scholarships, and the athlete just didn't turn out to be as good as the coaches projected him or her to be, that it was the coaches' responsibility and that they must honor the scholarship.

Unfortunately, there are not many athletic directors or coaches who operate that way. As a result, many athletes each year face the decision of returning to their school with no athletic scholarship, or with a smaller athletic scholarship, or must decide whether they should transfer to another school for a change of scenery and a fresh start.

Perhaps the most frustrating part of this type of situation for athletes and parents when a scholarship has been reduced or cancelled is this: If the athlete chooses to transfer to another institution, the coach and athletic department still have the right to approve or deny the athlete's opportunity to speak to other schools about the possibility of a transfer.

So, an athlete has their athletic scholarship reduced or cancelled and wants to speak to another school within the same conference or within the same state about the possibility of a transfer, but many times their school will not provide that opportunity. This scenario, and others like it, will be covered in the next chapter on Transfers.

Earlier in this chapter we discussed the difference between head-count sports and equivalency sports.

In equivalency sports, the coaches have the discretion divide their scholarships among their team members a choose, as long as the total number of scholarships provided does not exceed the maximum limit for their sport as prescribed by the NCAA (or by the NAIA, as appropriate).

The sport of NCAA Division I baseball has seen changes that place it in a bit of an unusual category. Unlike other equivalency sports, baseball must provide at least 25% scholarships to all new incoming student-athletes and must not have more than 27 "counters' on their roster. The following section discusses the new Division I baseball scholarship rules in more detail.

NCAA Division I Baseball Scholarship Rules

With the NCAA Division I baseball scholarship changes that became fully effective during the 2009-10 academic year, walk-ons will take on more important roles on baseball rosters. Each Division I institution will be limited to 27 counters (athletes receiving an athletic scholarship) among their roster limit of 35 players, with the other 8 spots being occupied by walk-ons who will receive no athletic scholarship.

Here are some situations that already have – or could – take place with the rules that became effective in Fall 2009:

1. Division I rosters of no more than 35 players must be established the day prior to the first contest in February. Coaches can have more than 35 players during the Fall and January practice periods, but must be at no more than 35 before the start of the season. Walk-ons who are on teams that have more than 35

players participating in fall practice sessions must be aware that they are at increased risk of being cut from the team. Once a player is cut from the team, he will not be able to use the athletic facilities to work out and will have no practice opportunities with the team.

2. A student-athlete who is receiving an athletic scholarship must be included in the counter limit of 27, and the total roster size of 35, even if they are injured and unable to play. So, a walk-on who has been performing well during practice sessions must be aware that they may be cut from the team to make room for an injured player receiving a scholarship because the injured player must be counted among the 27 and 35.

3. Juniors at Division I programs who choose to return to school for their senior year may be asked to return as a walk-on as their scholarship was probably already "given away" in the recruitment of an incoming freshman. This has already been the case for a number of years, but may become more common as the opportunity for coaches to give 5% or 10% scholarships to late signees is no longer available. This is because all new incoming baseball recruits, both freshmen and transfer, must now receive at least a 25% scholarship.

Some baseball programs have established their own set of "rules" for distributing scholarships. Some let recruits know up front that their scholarship will decline each year after their freshman year, while others may inform the players after their enrollment that there will not be a baseball scholarship for their senior year if they return.

Players and parents should be asking about the effect of the financial aid rules on their baseball scholarship so they will know well in advance.

For those who are walk-ons, especially at programs that have more than 35 players participating in Fall drills, it will be extremely important to assess your chances of making the 35-man roster that will be in effect for the season.

For those who choose to transfer, it is quite possible that a fresh start at an NCAA Division II or NAIA program may result in increased opportunities for financial aid, for playing time, and for a better opportunity to be drafted due to the increased playing time and more chances to be seen by scouts.

Team Scholarship Limits in Selected NCAA Sports:

NCAA Division I – Head Count Sports

Football – 85

Men's Basketball – 13

Women's Basketball – 15

Women's Gymnastics – 12

Women's Volleyball – 12

Women's Tennis – 8

NCAA Division I – Equivalency Sports

Baseball – 11.7 (and a maximum of 27 counters)

Softball – 12

Men's Cross Country/Track and Field – 12.6

Women's Cross Country/Track and Field – 18

Men's Gymnastics – 6.3

Men's Soccer – 9.9

Women's Soccer – 14

Men's Tennis – 4.5

Men's Volleyball – 4.5

Wrestling – 9.9

NCAA Division II – Equivalency Sports

Baseball – 9

Men's Basketball – 10

Women's Basketball – 10

Men's Cross Country/Track and Field – 12.6

Women's Cross Country/Track and Field – 12.6

Football – 36

Men's Soccer – 9

Women's Soccer – 9.9

Softball – 7.2

Men's Tennis – 4.5

Women's Tennis – 6

Men's Volleyball – 4.5

Women's Volleyball – 8

Wrestling - 9

Team Scholarship Limits in NAIA Sports:

Baseball – 12

Men's Basketball (Division I) – 11

Women's Basketball (Division I) – 11

Men's Basketball (Division II) – 6

Women's Basketball (Division II) – 6

Men's Cross Country – 5

Women's Cross Country – 5

Football – 24

Men's Golf – 5

Women's Golf – 5

Men's Soccer – 12

Women's Soccer – 12

Softball – 10

Men's Tennis – 5

Women's Tennis - 5

Men's Track and Field – 12

Women's Track and Field – 12

Volleyball – 8

Wrestling – 8

Team Scholarship Limits in Selected NJCAA Sports:

- <u>Division I JC's</u> may grant the number of scholarships listed here. Each Division I scholarship is limited to a maximum of tuition and fees, room and board, and required books.

- <u>Division II JC's</u> may grant the number of scholarships listed here, but Division II scholarships are limited to tuition, fees, and books.

- <u>Division III JC's</u> may not offer athletic scholarships.

- <u>California community colleges</u> are not governed by the NJCAA, and do not offer athletic scholarships.

Baseball – 24

Men's Basketball – 15

Women's Basketball – 15

Men's Cross Country - 10 (Combined with Half Marathon)

Women's Cross Country – 10 (Combined with Half Marathon)

Football – 85

Men's Golf - 8

Women's Golf – 8

Men's Soccer – 18

Women's Soccer – 18

Softball – 24

Men's Tennis – 9

Women's Tennis – 9

Note: NJCAA Division I tennis only allows 3 full scholarships - the other 6 may only be for tuition, fees and books.

Men's Track and Field – 20

Women's Track and Field – 20

Volleyball – 14

Wrestling - 16

Chapter Six – Transfer Information

"A bend in the road is not the end of the road...unless you fail to make the turn." Author Unknown

Many of my consultations with athletes and/or families have been concerning transferring to another school. These transfer situations can occur in a number of different ways, so I will summarize them into three categories, and share some stories of each.

The three main categories – in NCAA-speak – are 2-4 transfers (from a two-year school to a four-year school), 4-4 transfers (from a four-year school to another four-year school), and 4-2-4 transfers (from a four-year school, to a two-year school, and then on to a second four-year school).

2-4 Transfers

There are a number of reasons why an athlete starts out at a two-year school before transferring to a four-year school.

They may need to attend the two-year school to improve their academic status before transferring on to a four-year school, or they may choose to attend the two-year school first because it is less costly for them and their family.

Other athletes simply choose the two-year school because they have a better opportunity to play right away as a freshman, or they want to improve their strength and speed in order to have a better recruiting opportunity at a four-year school after attending the two-year school.

For a 2-4 transfer, the ability to transfer and be immediately eligible will be much easier if the student-athlete strives to meet the freshman academic eligibility requirements while in high school.

This was discussed in Chapter Four on Eligibility and I shared a couple of stories of 2-4 transfer situations from when I was in the Oklahoma State University athletic department.

The NCAA has increased the academic standards required for freshman eligibility at the Division I level and they are increasing the academic standards to be immediately eligible when transferring from a two-year college.

Student-athletes who were not certified as NCAA qualifiers upon completion of high school will be required to complete additional English and math courses at their two-year college in order to transfer from a two-year college and be immediately eligible for competition.

Also, from a recruiting standpoint, two-year college athletes should keep in mind that they will be recruited all over again, just as they were in high school. Or, in some cases, will NOT be recruited again similar to what happened to them in high school.

One of the athletes whom I have advised was not highly recruited out of high school, and also was not highly recruited when it was time to complete his Associates Degree and move on to a four-year college to continue his baseball career.

However, with perseverance, he did end up being recruited to an NCAA Division II university and receiving a scholarship for baseball, and was excited to have the opportunity to play.

4-4 Transfers

Many athletes and parents do not realize the control that NCAA institutions have over the process of a student-athlete transferring to another university, even when the coaches have reduced or cancelled an athletic scholarship.

A student-athlete cannot discuss the possibility of a transfer from a four-year college (NCAA or NAIA) to an NCAA Division I or II institution until they have been given permission by the college where they are currently enrolled.

This rule is in place to discourage institutions from "recruiting" student-athletes from other four-year colleges.

A student-athlete who contacts a coach at another college should be told by that coach that he or she cannot discuss the possibility of a transfer with the student-athlete until permission has been received from the college that the student-athlete is currently attending.

If permission is granted, most of the same recruiting rules that were in place during the athlete's high school recruitment will be in effect again.

In many cases, a student-athlete will be able to be immediately eligible at the school they are transferring to if permission is granted by their first institution, and if it is certified that they would have been academically eligible had they chosen to return to the college they were attending.

This option is not available for 4-4 baseball transfers to Division I programs, however.

Baseball 4-4 transfers going to a Division I institution will be required to attend the Division I program for one year before being eligible for competition, just as is the case for basketball or football transfers to Division I programs.

Most 4-4 transfers are smooth transitions from one college to another. Transfers become difficult situations if the athlete desires to transfer to a college that the first school does not want them to transfer to.

This is because NCAA schools have the right to deny permission for an athlete to speak to a particular school about the possibility of transfer. This difficulty is most common in situations in which the athlete desires to transfer within the same conference, or within the same state or region of the country.

From my years of experience at two large institutions, I believe that this usually occurs because the coaches do not want the athlete to have the opportunity to come back and compete against the school that they originally attended.

Often, the position of the coach at the first school is "We invested time and money in recruiting and training this athlete, so why would I allow them to go a school in the same conference and come back and compete against us?"

This past year, I consulted with the family of an athlete who desired to transfer from one university to another within the same conference.

The school denied the athlete's permission to speak to the other school about a possible transfer, and would not agree to the "one-time transfer rule."

I advised the athlete on the points that should be made in the letter to the Chairperson of the appeal committee, and the questions that the athlete should be prepared to answer in the actual appeal hearing. Unfortunately the appeal board upheld the athletic department decision and denied the athlete's appeal.

As a result, the athlete had to quickly develop a "Plan B" to find a school to transfer to and continue athletic competition.

A 4-4 transfer situation in which I was able to help the athlete obtain a positive outcome came in the sport of football when the athlete desired to transfer to another school for a better opportunity at a starting role.

The athlete was advised how best to approach the coach when meeting to request permission to speak to other schools.

The meeting resulted in a positive outcome and the opportunity to transfer in time for spring practice at the new school and be immediately eligible for the upcoming season.

-4 Transfers

These types of transfers seem to happen most often to baseball players. In most cases, the player does not get much playing time during their freshman year at a four-year college, and they choose to leave on their own.

In other cases, they are told by the coaching staff that they need to transfer in order to get more playing time because the coaching staff does not see a substantial role for them on their team in the future.

The two important points for athletes to consider in this situation are the opportunity to get substantial playing time, and making sure that the academic requirements are satisfied so that the athlete can be immediately eligible when transferring to the second four-year college.

If the athlete did not get much playing time as a freshman, they need to be aggressive about finding a place where they are virtually assured of substantial playing opportunities. This is especially true in the sport of baseball, and so once again, the player is in a situation where he is being recruited just as he was being recruited in high school.

However, in this case, it is more important that the athlete check out the two-year college and the coaches, than being concerned about the promises that are being made by the coaches.

What is the history of the program, how many players do they send on to four-year baseball programs, and what is the quality of programs that are recruiting players from this college? These are all questions that the athlete should be asking during the 4-2-4 transfer process.

It is equally important that the athlete make sure and know what they must do academically to be immediately eligible as a 4-2-4 transfer heading to the second four-year college.

Again, this is especially critical in baseball. This is because NCAA Division I programs have new transfer and eligibility rules to follow.

In the sport of Division I baseball, all players must be eligible at the start of the academic year.

Under the "old" set of rules, it was quite common for players to not be academically eligible at the start of the academic year in August or September. However, they could use the fall semester to "get well" and be academically eligible by the start of the spring semester in time for baseball season.

But, with the new rule in place, this is not an option as all athletes must be eligible at the start of the academic year if they are going to be able to play in the spring baseball season.

These baseball transfer rules in Division I do not allow an athlete to be eligible at midyear, even if they are transferring in from a two-year school and have graduated with an Associate's Degree.

It is very important to understand the academic transfer rules in this type of transfer situation.

The majority of my consultation with athletes and parents regarding 4-2-4 transfers has been ensuring that they know what they must do academically to be eligible upon transfer to the second four-year program.

This is especially important because in baseball, as well as basketball, new transfer rules have been enacted which severely limit the ability of an athlete to transfer in the middle of the academic year.

The timing of a transfer, and the academic requirements needed for a successful transfer can be complicated, as some rules require the completion of a two-year degree, or at least the successful completion of at least 12 hours of academic credit for each semester at the two-year college.

Also, the academic credits must be hours that will transfer to the new four-year program, so it is imperative to be taking courses that will count as transferable-degree credits.

A final note about transfers

During my time on campus, I regularly saw transcripts of transfers from two-year colleges who took a heavy load of physical education activity courses, such as weightlifting courses, or "Theory of Coaching Football," for example.

There were times when these athletes were not even close to being academically eligible for transfer from their two-year college.

This was because they could not satisfy the requirement that they have completed a specific percentage of their degree requirements for their chosen degree plan (40% by the third year of college, 60% by the fourth year, and 80% by the fifth year if they had eligibility remaining).

The example above is just another reminder of how important academics and course selection are in the eligibility process, or, more specifically, the transfer-eligibility process.

A Final Word...

With this book, I hope we have provided you with some insight & helpful information that will make your own recruiting or transfer situation easier.

Our son's collegiate baseball career is over & he is now a contributor & advisor with Informed Athlete. As a former college athlete, Ryan brings a unique point of view to Informed Athlete that only someone who has "been there" can understand. He provides input on website content and writing blogs & giving advice from the student athletes' perspective.

To learn more about our services, please contact me via email at rick@informedathlete.com, call our office at 918-994-7272 or visit www.informedathlete.com.

If you are the parent of a student-athlete, savor every moment as it's over way too soon. If you are a student-athlete, best of luck to you in reaching your goals!

Rick

Visit our website www.informedathlete.com
& subscribe to our **FREE** newsletter.

When you subscribe to our newsletter,
you will receive a copy of

***A Road Map for Playing at the College Level:
The Top 5 Questions to Consider***

To learn more about our services,
Please contact Rick Allen at 918-994-7272,
via e-mail at rick@informedathlete.com,
or visit www.informedathlete.com

Informed Athlete (www.informedathlete.com) offers education and advice regarding NCAA recruiting and eligibility rules, as well as athletic scholarships and many other issues.

This advice can be provided through various formats:

1. Blog topics on our website: www.informedathlete.com

2. FREE monthly newsletter that provides up-to-date information on NCAA rules, Q&A's on pertinent topics, current monthly recruiting calendars, and updates on upcoming events sent to our subscribers. (Go to www.informedathlete.com to sign up – your information and privacy will be protected and not shared with any other source.)

3. Group presentations in-person to high school athletes and/or parents *(Fee-based)*

4. One-on-one consultation with athletes and/or parents in person, via Skype or by phone *(Fee-based)*

5. Webinars and short-term classes that educate and discuss specific topics such as how to prepare for official visits, the importance of starting early, steps required for an athlete to transfer from one school to another, etc. *(Fee-based)*

6. FREE 20-30 minute interactive webcasts that discuss specific topics and/or interviews with coaches.

Sources:

www.ncaa.org

www.naia.org

www.njcaa.org

www.perfectgame.org

Made in the USA
Charleston, SC
23 July 2011